The Scholarship Game

A no-fluff guide to making college affordable

The
Scholarship Game

A no-fluff guide to making
college affordable

Luke Arnce

**COMPASS
BOOKS**

Winchester, UK
Washington, USA

First published by Compass Books, 2017
Compass Books is an imprint of John Hunt Publishing Ltd., Laurel House, Station Approach,
Alresford, Hants, SO24 9JH, UK
office1@jhpbooks.net
www.johnhuntpublishing.com
www.compass-books.net

For distributor details and how to order please visit the 'Ordering' section on our website.

Text copyright: Luke Arnce 2016

ISBN: 978 1 78279 419 6
978 1 78279 421 9 (ebook)
Library of Congress Control Number: 2016949327

A CIP catalogue record for this book is available from the British Library.

Design: Stuart Davies

Printed and bound by CPI Group (UK) Ltd, Croydon, CR0 4YY, UK

We operate a distinctive and ethical publishing philosophy in all
areas of our business, from our global network of authors to
production and worldwide distribution.

CONTENTS

Acknowledgments

To Ms. Nic and Grandpa Gardner. The help you two provided me during my application process was indispensable. Thank you.

1. Getting Started

When you mix hormone-addled teenage minds and major life decisions, the result is usually less than satisfactory. Unfortunately, these are the conditions present when you are forced to decide where to go to college, and the colleges don't make it any easier. They flood your mailbox with glossy brochures showing students smiling and laughing on grassy lawns and put so many facts and figures in your face that you feel like you're studying for some test. How are you, as you search for a place to spend the next four years of your life, supposed to cut through the college propaganda and determine where the grassy lawns are greenest? Additionally, how do you determine what colleges you can actually afford?

I know the feeling. I was also overwhelmed with the task of selecting a college. During the admission process, I applied to eighteen schools, wrote over twenty essays, and took part in sixteen interviews. It sucked. I would never wish such a tedious endeavor on my worst enemy. However, the ordeal gave me a lot of experience with many aspects of college admission. So, instead of annoying my friends with tidbits about college admission, I decided to write this book—a no-fluff guide to deciding where to apply, building college applications, and smoking college interviews and scholarship weekends written by a student for students. Just so you guys don't think I'm some random schmuck writing on a subject I know nothing about, I was able to win over $1,000,000 in school-specific scholarships, so my methods have had some success.

This book is a compilation of information and tips that I

picked up when I was going through the application process myself. It will address selecting colleges, filling out applications, and scholarship interviews along with some other stuff. Hopefully, it helps keep you from going insane during your application process. Please keep in mind throughout that I am by no means the law on this stuff. These are just tips and bits of information that I found useful, so if you don't agree with something I've said, you don't have to listen. Now that the disclaimer is out of the way let's get going. It's time to get you some application savvy so you can spend more time enjoying your senior year instead of sweating over your college applications.

2. Building Your Resume

As Sun Tzu once said, "Every battle is won or lost before it is ever fought." Well, Sun Tzu might as well have been writing a book on applying to college instead of military strategy because his advice is wholly applicable. If you wait until when you're applying to colleges to build your resume, you are a little late to the party. Most of the time, students participate in sports, band, or other extracurricular activities without thinking of their activities as part of their resume, so students can end up building their resume without thinking about it. However, it is a far better game plan to be intentional about designing your resume early so you aren't stuck piecing one together at the last minute. Starting your resume in your freshman year also helps you keep track of everything you've done, and it's better to be forced to pare down your resume than to be forced to rack your brain for other stuff you did just to fill the page.

Think of your resume as a candy bar with your GPA, ACT/SAT, and course difficulty as the plain chocolate exterior, and the extracurricular activities as the gooey, delicious center made of nougat and caramel. It's true; nobody's favorite part of the candy bar is the outside. It's just a housing for the tastiness in the middle, but nobody is going to eat a candy bar, no matter how delicious the middle is if the chocolate shell is moldy. A good ACT/SAT, a high GPA, and a difficult course load probably won't get you into the colleges you want by themselves, but a bad ACT/SAT, a low GPA, and four years of easy classes will get your application tossed. Does that mean you have to take hard classes, do your homework, and study for standardized tests?

Yes, it does. Also, if you aren't interested in the hardest classes at your school, but you could do well in them, suck it up and take them. You can be picky with your courses in college, but in high school you need to take the classes that show colleges you have the academic chops to handle college level courses.

Excluding of your ACT/SAT, GPA, and course difficulty, the rest of your resume should showcase accomplishment, leadership, motivation, and service, so find activities that fit the criteria and participate in them. Try to participate in activities you're interested in, but also, try some things you might not like. Stretch yourself. Even if you hate every minute of it and decide never to do it again, you can still put it on your resume.

The easiest way to start participating in activities you can put on your resume is through your high school. High school's typically have a variety of clubs or programs for students like student council, football, choir, and FBLA. Some of these programs call for a major time commitment. However, others require almost none even if you're in a leadership position, so do a little reconnaissance on the clubs you plan on joining. Try to participate in activities you're really interested in, but also join a few clubs that require little time commitment that might not be intriguing to you. You might end up liking a few more than you thought, and the others will just show that you've made an effort to determine your interests.

Another thing colleges will love, even if you don't, is leadership positions, so run for as many as you can handle. *But running for offices is scary.* Well, tough. High school is where you're going to get most, if not all, of your leadership positions for your resume, so you're just going to have to grit your teeth and do it. If you lose the election, nobody will care or remember. Even if they do, you probably won't see them after high school anyways. Also, keep in mind that not all leadership positions are created equal. There is president, and then everything else, so, unless you don't think you can win the presidential election, run for president. If you do end up running for some other office, make sure it's the office with the least opposition because all offices besides president are the same in the eyes of colleges. Keep in mind that colleges won't know how many students are in the clubs at your school, so whether you're president of a club with six people or sixty, all your resume will say is club president.

Community service should also be on your mind as you craft your resume. You don't necessarily have to go out and be a modern Mother Teresa unless service is something you're passionate about, but you do need to show you aren't a cold-hearted jerk with no concern for others. Besides looking good on your resume, service can actually help change your perspective on life. Serving people who are less fortunate than you can give you a better appreciation for what life has given you. However, this is a book on crushing your college applications, not squishy feelings, so let's get back to putting service on your resume. Some go-to options for community service are soup kitchens and after-school tutoring programs. Sometimes, schools even have community service student organizations, which provide opportunities for students to serve in various ways. Community service is also required for select scholarships and entrance into some honor societies, so you can find several opportunities to double dip by getting service hours for your resume and something else. Make sure to keep track of your hours of community service, because many schools will ask you to list hours of service. Well, I've sufficiently sucked the altruism out of volunteering; I feel like taking a bath.

Besides volunteering and accumulating leadership positions, you should also focus on amassing accolades to showcase your talents. If everyone at your school knows you're a world-class opera singer, but you've never performed on stage or entered any competitions, your talent won't be communicated in your resume. Show off your talent by entering relevant competitions.

Otherwise, colleges will assume you don't have the talent. If you're good at something that has a club or team at school, join the club and go to the competitions, but go beyond that. Say you're good at art, for example. Yes, enter all the local contests and showcases your art class at school participates in. Do some research; find state and national contests to enter your art in as well. Not only do the outside contests help showcase your talent, but they also show you have the initiative to succeed on your own.

In fact, showing initiative and growth is a major part of building a strong resume. Colleges want to admit students with upward trends—students who improved their grades and became more involved as high school went on. The primary method for showing initiative on your resume is to participate in school activities. Don't stop there, though. Go beyond and find projects to work on outside of school, like the competitions in the art example. You can also show initiative by interning or volunteering at a business or in a college department you're interested in. Don't worry. Getting involved in a business or college department isn't as difficult as it first seems. Just ask. People outside of high school aren't going to actively recruit students to their businesses or departments, so you're going to have to be proactive. Send the professors you want to work with an email about your interest or stop by the business you're interested in to see if you can volunteer for them. They might let you get involved, and if they don't, you can just ask someone else. The only thing that's certain is if you don't ask, you won't receive.

Another aspect of your resume that might be worthwhile to develop is hidden extracurricular activities. Something would be categorized as a hidden extracurricular activity if it doesn't fit well anywhere else on your resume, but it provides interesting insight into you as a person. These types of activities help pique the interest of the admissions officer who's trying not to fall asleep after reading his third application in a row with Model

U.N., Student Council, and French Club. Try to make sure the hidden extracurriculars you include are more like, "taught myself Swedish" or "personally developed a diversified stock portfolio with a 200% return" not "casual Halo gamer" or "lover of many television shows." If it doesn't make you look good, don't include it.

By building your resume with leadership, accolades, community service, extra-scholastic activities, and a few hidden extracurriculars in mind, you will have a strong resume. However, for a resume that puts you in the running for big merit scholarships or intrigues the admissions officers at even the snootiest schools, you're going to need some extra oomph. In order to make your resume stellar, you'll need at least two or three hook activities—activities that make whoever is reading your application call their co-workers over to look at. These activities do need to be related to your interests because they will probably take up a lot of your time. Activities like running your own business, writing music and getting it published, filing for a patent, starring in a play that people who aren't related to you pay to see, or placing in the top ten in a national competition are great. To compile activities and accomplishments at this level, you have to buckle down and do the hard work. However, if you can reach those goals, or even get close to those goals, not only will your resume be dynamite, but you will uncover determination and ability you never knew you had.

What you want to show schools with your resume is that you've been successful in the high school environment, but you had a thirst for more that drove you to participate in activities outside of school. Now, you're ready to break out of the constraining cocoon of high school, and flutter like the well-rounded butterfly you are onto a college campus. You can do it. You can be the butterfly. Just work hard and record your activities as you go along. Then, you won't have the added stress of trying to remember everything you've done in high school while trying to figure out where you want to apply, which is an arduous ordeal in its own right.

3. Selecting Colleges

Now that you've crafted a superb resume, you need to decide which colleges you want to send it to. There are over 4,000 two or four-year colleges in the United States alone, so to efficiently determine which schools you're interested in, you need to establish personalized criteria for selecting schools. Let's start off with some bad reasons to apply or not apply to a particular college.

1. Applying to a school because your friends are. Yes, it's easier to enter a foreign environment with some familiar faces, but just because it's easy or convenient doesn't mean it's the right decision. Will the fact that you have friends on campus make your first lunch in the cafeteria less awkward? Yes. Will the fact that you followed your friends to a school that doesn't offer a major in computer science hurt your chances of becoming a software engineer at Google like you always wanted? Undoubtedly. Remember, the primary function of college is to give you perspective, and prepare you for a career, not to provide a place for you and your high school buddies to retell old stories. By hanging out with your friends from high school in college, you're depriving yourself of the opportunity to meet other interesting people who don't remember that time you accidentally called Mrs. Thompson, "Mom."

2. Avoiding applying to a school because it looks too expensive. A school's sticker price can be misleading.

Often, the most expensive schools are also the most generous. In many circumstances, attending a university with a ridiculous sticker price like Harvard or Yale is more affordable than attending a local university with a low sticker price, particularly if you're in a low socioeconomic group. Stanford now guarantees that if a student's family makes less than $125,000, they will pay no tuition, and many other elite institutions are now making similar offers. So before eliminating a school from your application list because you assume you won't be able to afford attending or applying to a school because you think it will be cheap, complete the online net price calculator provided by the school. You might be surprised.

3. Applying to schools because they send you tons of mail. This may sound a little ridiculous at first, but don't be surprised if you find yourself holding one of the school's postcards midway through application season and thinking, "I know everything about this school is wrong for me, but I just appreciate their tenacity. Maybe I should give them another look." Don't do it. Put that postcard in the trash with the thirty others they sent you last week. Don't let your stalker schools wear you down. You would never date a stalker just because they always seem to be around and interested in you, so don't apply to a stalker school for the same reason. If the schools weren't right for you when you first looked, don't allow their never-ending streams of mail to make them seem more attractive.

4. Applying to a school because it is highly ranked. Just because a school is highly ranked, doesn't mean the school is a good fit for you. It's easy just to look at the rankings and base your applications on someone else's opinion, but you're not finding the schools that are best for you. The

methodology you use to select schools is going to be different than the methodology *U.S. News* and *World Report* uses, and that's how it should be. Allow what you find important in a school to direct your search.

5. Applying to college because you think it's the next thing to do. College is a major investment of time and money. Don't waste your time if you don't have a good reason for going. Going to college because you want to make more money, is a valid reason to attend, because, on average, those who graduated from college make more money than those who didn't. Wanting to learn and experience life in a different environment also makes college a good option for you. College campuses are melting pots of ideas and customs from around the world, which provides students with the chance to see how others formulate ideas and act. College is also helpful if you're following a passion. To conduct the Boston Symphony Orchestra or perform brain surgery, you're going to have to go through some college. There's no way around it. Those are all good reasons for attending college. However, if you're going to college because you want to party, your parents want you to, you don't know what else to do, or something else along those lines, you might end up with a mountain of student loan debt and nothing to show for it.

Once you know you want to attend college, many factors go into determining where you want to apply. For starters, you need to decide where, geographically speaking, you want to go to school. If the mere thought of living in frigid temperatures makes you look for the nearest bridge, do not apply to schools in northern Minnesota. Additionally, if the thought of missing your Mom's next birthday makes you cry through two boxes of tissues, don't apply to schools far away from home. If where you live for the next four years is important to you, make location a factor in determining where to apply. There is no sense in applying to a school in a location you know you will hate.

Determining what student body size you're comfortable with is another important step in refining your college search. To some students, attending a university with 40,000 students sounds intimidating and overwhelming, while other students think attending a school with a population under 5,000 would be boring and restricting. Neither position is inherently wrong, and each environment has certain benefits and drawbacks. Schools with tons of students usually have a wide range of student organizations. Take Ohio State University, for example. OSU has one of the highest student populations in the country, and it has over 1,000 clubs. Conversely, small schools often provide exemplary one-on-one attention to students. Williams College, a liberal arts college in Massachusetts with just over 2,000 students, has a student-faculty ratio of 7 to 1. Huge universities also tend to party huge, and while some small schools are also known for parties (*cough cough* Dartmouth) most small schools don't party as hard as their gigantic counterparts. Both extremes present different environments, but if you don't care what size the school is, don't eliminate schools based on size. Narrow your college list down with other criteria you care about.

If you already know what you want to major in or know what subject you're interested in, you can use that information to help narrow your college search. Say you know you want to be an aerospace engineer. Make sure you apply to schools that have an aerospace engineering major. It's not rocket science; well, actually aerospace engineering often is, but that's not the point. Even if you aren't completely sure what you want to do, if you're hard set on a field like engineering, you can still use that information to whittle down your list of colleges. Do not, however, choose a school based on a specific major if you don't know what you want to do. Ending up at a school primarily for engineers if your true passion is dancing is going to leave you dancing with yourself.

Should you have the opportunity, school visits are also very useful when deciding where to apply. Although you can find a great deal of information about most schools online, it's hard to replace checking the school out for yourself. The school may look fantastic on paper, but the students may be a bunch of pretentious jerks who would make your life miserable, and that's hard to glean from a website. If you do get the opportunity to visit schools, don't just go on the tour. To get a good sense of what the school is actually like, you need to talk with the students. Ask them what they like about the school, what they don't like, what they would change, and anything else you're interested in knowing. This is your chance to get raw feedback from real students instead of the fluffy testimonies colleges put on their websites. Go to a class, provided your schedule allows. You might not understand anything the professor is talking about, but it gives you an opportunity to see how the teachers and students interact with each other. Overnight programs are also excellent for experiencing what everyday life would be like at a specific college. Many overnight programs leave parts of the day unscheduled, so you can spend time walking around campus, checking out club activities, or playing World of Warcraft in your host's dorm room. Essentially, the more time you spend at a particular school, the better your understanding of what life at that school would be like.

The most important factor in determining if a college is right for you is whether or not the school is affordable for you. Even if everything else about the school is exactly what you're looking for, if you aren't comfortable paying or are unable to pay the cost of attendance, the school isn't a good fit for you. Because of this, the importance of understanding your financial situation cannot be stressed enough. Before you start looking at colleges, you need to have a candid conversation with your parents about paying for college. You need to know if your family is going to contribute to the cost of your college, and, if so, how much. Money is often an uncomfortable subject to discuss, so make sure to approach the conversation tactfully. Try to communicate that by having a complete understanding of your financial situation, you can more accurately determine where to send your applications, which will save money and time that would have been wasted on applications to schools that weren't affordable to you.

Unfortunately, your parents are going to have to do a little more than just tell you the amount they're willing to contribute to your education. Okay, a lot more, and it is going to suck big time. So, if you want to know whether you will be able to afford a particular school or not, you're going to have to bake them some cookies and not pipe off when they whine over and over again about how much they hate filling out the net price calculator. One way to make filling out net price calculators a little less painful for you and your parents is first to complete The College Board's Net Price Calculator. This Calculator provides net cost of attendance for over 200 schools, so if you're interested in any of the net price calculator's participating colleges, using it can save you and your parents a lot of time and headache. The chances are, however, that some of the schools you're looking at won't be members of College Board's Net Price Calculator, so you'll have to fill out individual net price calculators for each school. *Well, this is a huge pain.* Yes, it is, but you can make it less painful by recording the information you input into the first net price calculator you complete in a word document. That way, you can input the information faster, and you don't have to force one of your parents to do it every time. The work is put squarely on your shoulders, but you don't have to wait for your parents to get in the form-completing mood.

Net cost could be a primary concern to you, so you will probably want net cost to be a factor early on in helping you select colleges. You can usually approximate what need-based financial aid a college is going to give you with your socioeconomic standing. If your family is lower class to middle class, schools that meet 100% of demonstrated need will be exceedingly generous to you. So generous, in fact, that if your family makes less than $60,000 a year you can go to Harvard, Yale, Stanford, Duke, and similar schools completely free. Consider it life's penance for kicking you in the teeth. A great place to start looking for schools that will give you a lot of money would be lists online of schools that meet 100% of demonstrated need. These schools range from highly selective schools like Princeton, Yale, and CalTech, to less selective schools like Bethany College in Kansas and Thomas Aquinas College in California, so your options are wide open. However, if you want to broaden your search to schools with higher acceptance rates but want to maintain affordability, try looking at schools that meet 80% of demonstrated need. These schools also provide great aid to students who qualify while admitting a higher percentage of students.

This paragraph is going to make upper middle-class kids a little unhappy, so, if that's you, steel yourself for some dream-stomping. Upper middle-class students are, sadly, in the donut hole of paying for college. Your family makes too much for you to receive need-based aid, but your family doesn't make enough to write off the ridiculous price of some college educations. Unfortunately, the colleges that meet 100% of demonstrated financial need offer very few, if any, merit-based scholarships. That means no matter how fantastic you are as a student, if you're from an upper middle-class family you can't go to Harvard, Yale, Princeton or other similar schools if your family isn't willing to pay $65,000 a year. If you're interested in a school like Harvard, by all means, fill out the net price calculator, because everybody's circumstance is different, and you might get money. However, don't think that the school is magically going to decide to give you thousands of dollars if you fill out the net price calculator and you get nothing. The net price calculators are fairly accurate, and if you decide to apply despite the net price calculator saying you won't get anything, the worst possible circumstance might occur. You might get in. Then you're going to be mad at everybody because you got in, but they will cover none of your $65,000 cost of attendance.

Don't despair upper middle-class kids. Not all hope is lost. You're just going to have to look at schools with merit-based scholarships to help cover your costs. While students from lower income families will look at lists of schools that meet 100% of financial need, you need to look at lists of schools that provide the most merit-based aid. Much like the schools that meet 100% of demonstrated need, there is a variety of schools represented. Lesser known liberal arts colleges like Centre, Hendrix, and Wooster are represented, but so are a few name-brand schools like Duke, Vanderbilt, and Georgetown. Unfortunately, merit scholarships are difficult to get. Not only do you have to get accepted to the university, but you also have to be one of the top students admitted.

Though socioeconomics plays a large part in choosing where to apply when considering cost, there is a small group of schools that would appeal to cost conscientious students of all socioeconomic classes—tuition-free colleges. Tuition-free institutions such as College of the Ozarks and Alice Lloyd College, pay students through campus jobs. Others, namely the United States Service Academies including the United States Naval Academy and West Point, pay students with years of service after graduation. The service academies also cover room and board for all students.

While merit scholarships are probably most desperately needed by upper middle-class kids who aren't receiving much financial support from their families, merit scholarships are beneficial for all students regardless of socioeconomic status. For some reason, schools usually don't like to advertise their merit scholarships. If the school provides any merit scholarships, they will most likely be listed somewhere deep in the recesses of the school website. Instead of wasting your time clicking through useless pages, just type "School X merit scholarships" into Google. You'll skip the unneeded frustration of trying to find the scholarships by navigating through only the school's website.

Once you find the scholarships, read about them. Find out how many scholarships are awarded, see if you meet the minimum ACT/SAT and GPA requirements, and read about what you need to do to qualify for the scholarship. Some scholarships require additional essays and other supplementary information to be submitted for a student to be considered, so be prepared for some extra writing. Also, try to find information about the past scholarship winners to give you a better understanding of the competitiveness of the scholarship. Once you understand the level of competition for the scholarship, you will have a better understanding of your chances of winning the scholarship, which will give you a more accurate projection of the school's cost to you.

When making the final decisions on where you're going to apply, it's important to keep your options open. Treat your college applications like pruning a tree. You want to cut the dead, damaged, and diseased branches away. Otherwise, they will get in the way and prevent the healthy branches from getting enough sunlight. They might even spread disease to the healthy branches. However, if you cut too many branches away, then the tree won't be able to gather enough nutrients to support itself, and it will die. Don't apply to a ton of schools you aren't interested in, because it will give you less time to focus on the schools you care about, and your applications will suffer. On the other hand, however, don't apply to just one or two schools because you might not get as much money as you thought you would, and if you only applied to a couple schools, you don't have very many extra options. Just make sure you have enough branches to keep your tree alive, but not so many branches that the good branches can't get any nutrients. If paying for application fees worries you, don't sweat it. Most colleges will provide application fee waivers for you if you let them know you need help paying the fee.

An important step in ensuring you are applying to a variety of schools is to establish a tiered structure. You don't necessarily need to apply to a variety of schools as in small vs. big, private vs. public, or close to home vs. far away. The variety you need to establish in the schools you apply to is the chance of you being able to afford attending. That means you're going to need a healthy mix of safety schools, match schools, and reach schools.

Safety schools are schools that you know you will get accepted to and know you will be able to afford. These schools are often local universities or community colleges, which tend to make decisions on scholarships significantly earlier than more selective schools, which means you will know what these schools will offer you first. Just because a school is one of your safety schools doesn't mean you should dislike the school. Try to find schools you could easily get into and afford that you would enjoy attending for your safety schools. Some of your safety schools might not have everything you want in a college, but you should still feel comfortable with attending any of the schools you choose to apply to. If you can't imagine yourself attending a school, don't apply to it. You end up attending that school and you will be a jerk to other students, the faculty, and yourself which will prevent you from benefiting fully from the school's academic resources. Plus, everybody will think you're a stuck up tool, so your social life will suck.

Match schools are the schools you will probably get into and be able to afford. Most of the schools you apply to should be match schools because these are the schools that fit what you are looking for in a college and will probably make the cost of attendance affordable for you. What types of schools you select as match schools will probably be determined by your financial situation. For those in lower socioeconomic groups, match schools should consist of schools that you will probably get into that will meet your financial need with aid and schools that you know you will get into and be able to afford by combining merit scholarships you will probably get and need-based financial aid. If you're upper middle-class, your match schools should be schools that you know you will get into that offer merit scholarships that you would probably win that would make attending affordable or schools that you will get into and be able to attend without financial aid.

Reach schools are schools that you probably won't be able to afford or get accepted to. These schools should represent where you would go if you got accepted everywhere and money wasn't an obstacle. That being said, affording your reach schools needs to be at least remotely attainable, which isn't a problem if are a part of a low socioeconomic group. Many school's students consider reach schools to offer generous need-based financial aid. However, if your family is upper middle-class, you would have no chance of affording several typical reach schools including all of the Ivy League. Of course, complete the net price calculator on the school website before completely ruling it out, but, again, if the cost of attendance is still too high, don't expect it to change if you get accepted. Your reach schools will have to consist of schools with highly competitive merit scholarships programs, which can include state schools like Michigan, UC Berkeley, UVA, and UNC-Chapel Hill, private liberal arts colleges including Kenyon, Denison, and Rhodes, or even a few name-brand schools like Emory and WashU in St. Louis.

When you're a senior in high school, it seems like every college is pulling you in a different direction, and there are too many colleges for you to start sorting through them without a game plan, so, before you start deciding where you'll submit applications, you need to establish criteria for selecting where you want to apply. Establish the criteria that are important to you and find colleges that match what you are looking for. Once you've found colleges that match your criteria, organize them into safety, match, or reach schools depending on your chance of acceptance and the school's affordability to you. By organizing your college search, you can determine where you want to apply quickly and efficiently, so you have time for a well-deserved nap before you actually start completing your applications. If you thought deciding where to apply was difficult, you might want to grab a stuffed animal or something because the real pain is about to start.

4. Deciding when to Apply

Before you jump right into filling out your applications, you need to get organized. There are too many different deadlines for you to start completing stuff willy-nilly, so before you start filling out application information, you need to know several important bits of information for each school you're applying to. You need to know the early decision, early action, and regular decision application deadlines, you need to know the FAFSA and CSS Profile deadlines, you need to know the deadlines for submitting your ACT/SAT scores, and you need to know if the college requires an interview, and if so, you need to know the deadline for scheduling one. A great way to keep all of these dates organized without tattooing them on your arm is to find a college application checklist online, print it out, and fill it with your college deadlines. If you check it regularly, an application checklist will help keep deadlines from creeping up on you.

Early on in completing your applications, you need to decide whether you want to apply Early Decision, Early Action, or Regular Decision to your colleges. Let's go over what those terms mean, in case you haven't heard them before.

Early Decision is essentially proposing to a college. The college still has the chance to reject you, but, if they accept you, you're pretty much locked in. By applying early decision, you're telling the college they are your first choice. It might get you over the hump if you're a borderline applicant, but don't apply Early Decision to a college unless you are totally sure you will go there if you are accepted, especially if finances might be an issue because if you get into your ED school, you won't be able to consider financial packages from other schools. If you do decide to apply to a school ED, make sure you're either filthy rich or know the school will cover your cost because of your financial need. Also, if you apply ED to a college, you still need to work the rest of your college applications while you're waiting to hear back, because if it isn't good news and you haven't worked on your other apps, you're going to have a lot of catching up to do.

Early Action is a cross between Early Decision and Regular Decision, because your application is due earlier, and you are notified of the college's decision earlier, but the application is non-binding. You can still consider other schools if you get in. If your application is ready by a school's Early Action deadline, go ahead and submit it, because it will be in a smaller pool of applicants, and you won't be locked into the school. However, if you feel like you need more time to make your test scores or extracurriculars on your application stronger, hold off on applying until Regular Decision.

Regular Decision is when most college applicants apply. Mainly because high school students procrastinate, but also because it gives applicants the most amount of time to perfect their applications. Since regular decision is the largest applicant pool, the competition is a little tougher, but this decision option, like early action, is non-binding, so you can send regular decision applications everywhere without any college feeling jilted.

Rolling Admission is another admission system some colleges use. Rolling Admission allows potential students to submit their application in a large window of time, usually from early fall to mid-summer. Because of the extended application window, these schools are good options if you need to apply somewhere else last minute. You do have a better chance of getting accepted to a school with Rolling Admission if you apply early, but typically schools with rolling admission admit a high percentage of applicants, so you'll probably, still have a good chance of getting accepted if you apply late.

Besides knowing what admission option you're going to pick for each school you're applying to, you need to think about the tone of your applications before you move on. Remember, even though most applications are completed online, your audience will not be impressed by an application that uses Twitter or Facebook grammar and spelling. You may think spelling words with numbers is gr8, but you're trying to present yourself as a mature, learned individual who would be a credit to the university, so stop writing like a preteen.

5. Activities List

The first part of your application you complete should be the activities list. Hopefully, you've already been building the basis of this section by developing a resume, but if you haven't don't worry too much, because even if you have a resume at this point, you're still going to have to do some restructuring to make it fit the CommonApp Activities List. Not all schools are on the CommonApp, however, most of the schools you will apply to probably are, so this section will be specifically about the activity list on the CommonApp. Although, don't skip this section if you aren't applying to schools on the CommonApp because other applications have similar sections, and most of the material covered will still be applicable.

Don't send a resume unless a school specifically asks for one. Even if you already have a resume done, and you don't want to fill out the activities list, don't do it. Admissions counselors find it annoying, and annoying the people who decide whether you get accepted or rejected is a bad decision. The activity list was developed so students wouldn't have to submit resumes and admissions counselors wouldn't have to read them, so if you send a resume anyway, it looks like you don't agree with or respect what they want from applicants. You can certainly use your resume to help build your activities list, but, don't send your resume to a school that doesn't want it. Seriously, submit what the school wants.

The CommonApp has ten slots for activities, so if you have more than that you're going to have to decide which activities will make the cut. You want to keep the activities you're still involved in and either sound impressive or actually are impressive, and drop the stuff that you aren't involved in anymore or just isn't that impressive. If you were a part of the Junior Varsity Croquet team your freshman year and didn't participate after that, you shouldn't put that on your activity list in place of something else. In fact, you probably just shouldn't put that on there even if you have space. Don't try to fill all ten spots so that you don't have any blanks. Include the activities you're passionate about and avoid cluttering your activities list with things like, "Designated paper stapler in Mrs. Simmons class." Honestly, the admissions staff thinks that is even less impressive than you do.

When filling out the activities list, keep in mind space is precious. You're only given 150 characters to present details, awards, and honors about each activity, so don't allow yourself to waste any with clunky wording. Precede your accomplishments with action verbs to keep your information pertinent and your presentation succinct, and don't reuse the same verbs for each activity. Try to maintain a little variety in your diction. Maybe instead of writing, "led an effort to…" you could say, "spearheaded an effort to…" or instead of, "started a new…" you could say, "established a new…" The alterations may seem minute, but if you were an admissions officer, would you rather admit someone who has led several teams, or someone who has directed, mentored, and supervised different teams?

The admissions committee is going to be presented with a plethora of excellent applications, so you need to make sure your application is as strong as it possibly can be. Admissions counselors are human, which is for the best because students are more than test scores and GPAs. However, because admissions counselors are human, your application won't be judged on your achievements, but how the committee perceives your achievements. That means you need to pay particular attention to how you word your accomplishments on your activities list. Make sure to tell them as much of the good information as you can, and leave out all of the bad information. If you got second place in a state ventriloquism competition, that's great. Put "Second in State Ventriloquism Competition" on your activities list. Don't, however, say, "Placed second out of two entries with a score of 30 out of 100." That information doesn't help you. You should avoid including information that will make your accomplishment less impressive if you can. Don't lie about your placements or awards, but don't use up space on your activities list making your accomplishments less impressive.

If you didn't have enough room to talk about all of your accomplishments in competitive juggling, or whatever on your activities list, don't worry. You can put the rest in the additional information section. The additional information section acts as a catch-all for the CommonApp. If you want the admissions team to know something, and it didn't fit elsewhere you should put it here. Don't just fill this section with fluff because it is additional. If you're going to make an admissions officer read more than they already have to normally, that information had better not be a bunch of junk they didn't need to know. Otherwise, they will be ticked off. There are several circumstances, however, when the additional information section should be utilized. For example, if you need to include important details about your activities that didn't fit on the activities list. Just make sure you keep it short and sweet. Use bullet points, and don't write in complete sentences. Just say what is important, and then move on. If there are AP test scores or other test scores you didn't put elsewhere, this is also a good section to list them.

You can also use this section to explain any red flags on your application. For example, if the reason your grades the second semester of your sophomore year were trash is because you had open heart surgery and you were stuck in the hospital for three months, this would be a good spot to let the admissions team know. Don't use this section to whine about a mean teacher who

gave you a bad grade. Make sure you're providing an explanation and not an excuse. Also, if the reason you got a D+ in
Calculus was because you were super lazy, don't explain that in
the additional information section. You can also include learning
disabilities, parental unemployment, and anything else that
would have made it harder for you to do well in school or get
involved in extracurricular activities. For example, if you had to
work thirty hours a week to help support your family, that would
definitely fit in this section. Remember to pay attention to your
tone. You want to provide an explanation, not an excuse.

If you have space left, but you're struggling to think of things
to write, stop writing. Don't feel obligated to fill up all the space.
Once you've included what you think the admissions counselors
would find helpful, stop writing and move on to the next part of
your applications.

6. Essays

While it can be difficult to put creative flair into your activities list, it is essential in your application essays. Your essay should show the admissions team what an interesting person you are. William Zinger in *On Writing Well* said, "Ultimately, the product that any writer has to sell is not the subject being written about, but who he or she is." Use your essay to communicate what no other section of your application can—your personality. You should use your essay to distil your motivations and thought processes into a power-packed 250 to 600 words of raw, self-revealing goodness. Don't freak out. It's actually not that bad once you know what you're doing, so let's get started.

Don't change your writing style to try to make yourself sound more intelligent. Your reader is probably not going to be wielding a red pen and slashing thick lines through little grammatical errors in your essay while laughing diabolically. In fact, it's more likely they're curled up on their couch drinking coffee and reading applications in their PJs, so don't write your application essay like an AP Literature essay. Your reader isn't looking for esoteric verbiage and flawless composition. Personal essays are included in applications because, when written well, they provide views into a student's life and personality, so unless you normally use super high diction, saying stuff like, "I was sentient, not somnambulant, so I walked brusquely past the edifice" makes you look like a second grader paging through a thesaurus looking for big synonyms.

You should also avoid writing about something you've already covered in another part of your application. Do not use your essay to relist everything you were involved in and achieved in high school. Yes, the admissions team knows you were in chess club and Spanish club and coffee club because you already told them, so move on. The more often the admissions officer reads about something you've done on your application, the less impressed by it they will be. If you absolutely feel you have to write an essay about something you've covered already and nothing anyone says will stop you, then write about a specific aspect of your activity and focus on communicating your thoughts about how the activity has affected you.

Some schools will want you to write an additional essay, usually asking, "Why us?" Avoid responding with a generic essay that doesn't talk about why you actually like that particular school. The admissions officers are not going to be impressed with one-size-fits-all statements like, "It's pretty" or, "The teachers are good." You're not fooling anyone with generic statements like those, and the admissions officers will interpret your lack of real reasons as a lack of real interest. List specific reasons for why you would like to attend. Talk about how a particular professor's research is intriguing to you, and you would like to get involved in his research, or express your interest in a unique major offered by the school. If you can't think of anything specific you like about the school, stop being lazy. Look on the web page and find something, and not just some piddly factoid you found in two seconds. Look hard. The extra time it takes to find real reasons you're interested in a school will be worth it.

Another essay pitfall you should try to avoid is picking a cliche topic. Please, for the love of admissions counselors everywhere, do not use one of these hackneyed topics:

The "I did community service once, and it taught me helping people is good" essay.

Writing about that one time you built a house in Morocco and it taught you the importance of service is great, as long as you can talk about how you became deeply involved in many community service projects afterward. If you didn't get more involved in service projects after you realized service was good, you're kind of undermining what you said you learned.

The "I played sports, and it taught me to work hard" essay.

This is the essay everyone who ever played sports will write, and it is rarely ever interesting. By talking about how you or your team practiced hard and won the big game, or how you or your team lost but then you worked hard and eventually won, you are wasting an opportunity to differentiate yourself from other applicants.

The "I went to a different country, and it's different than the US" essay.

Talking about how you went to another country and had to adapt to its culture doesn't showcase anything about you because anyone would be forced to adapt. If you're dead set on writing about your experience in a foreign country, keep the essay focused on you. After all, you're trying to sell...promote yourself, not some exotic location.

Those are a few common essay topics that you should try to avoid, but there are plenty others to avoid as well. It is generally a bad idea to use one of the mentioned topics because everyone uses them, but, you might use it anyways. If you do, you have to twist it. You can't write a typical essay if you're going to use a typical topic, so make sure you "wow" them with your writing skill or the events that take place.

When writing your essay, don't try to be somebody you aren't. Again, the primary purpose of the admissions essays is to provide the admissions counselors a glimpse of you as beyond a list of accomplishments and involvement. If you try to present a fake version of yourself in your essays, the writing will come off as shallow and uninspired, so let your actual voice come through. It's not a big deal if your thoughts aren't always about the welfare of humanity or building intergalactic satellites because that's not what most people think about constantly anyways. Present yourself unashamedly as who you are, and you will connect with your reader.

The best college essays elicit emotional responses, by connecting with your reader. Sure, you can get by with an essay that isn't particularly moving, but, if you want a home run, you're going to have to get your reader involved. You want your essay to make them laugh, cry, or cheer. Better yet, make them do all three. If your essay is poignant, emphasize the somber tone by utilizing a few well-placed abrupt sentences and simple sentence structures. If you're trying to be funny, don't spend the entire essay making jokes. Be comical in your description of the scenario. Whatever you write, try get some emotional response from your reader. By making them laugh, cry, or cheer in the middle of their office like a goofball, you are increasing your chances of being remembered.

Some colleges, like Stanford and Hendrix, require students to answer several short response questions. Honestly, dealing with short response questions is a pain, because you have to treat the short response questions like the essay questions. You can't just jot some random answer down and expect to do well; you have to think about the questions. As with the essays, your short responses shouldn't repeat information you've already said. However, the short response questions do provide students with an opportunity to show some flair more readily than most essay questions would, so don't give lame answers.

Here's an example of some kid being a square:

Name your favorite books, authors, films, and/or musical artists.
"1984, War and Peace, Shakespeare, Citizen Kane, and

Beethoven."

Even if dense prose gets your juices flowing, you need to inject a little variety, and truth, into your answer. The admissions counselors aren't going to crucify you if you like something lighthearted. In fact, they will probably appreciate your honesty.

Here's a better list:

Name your favorite books, authors, films, and/or musical artists.
"1984, Monty Python and the Holy Grail, Beethoven, and Beethoven's contemporary, Taylor Swift."

The answer still shows some intellect, but it also reveals the applicant is human and has some mundane interests. Ironically, showing you have some typical interests will actually make your application more interesting, because most people will use their answers to try to further impress the admissions officers.

When writing your application essays, keep in mind your readers do not know you. They don't know that when you say, "I'm okay at the bagpipes" you really mean, "I've won several international bagpipe competitions." Your essay is not the place to be overly humble. Don't be prideful, but would a bikini model looking for work send pictures of herself donning a winter coat to potential employers? No. Then why should you smother your talents with misplaced humility when writing application essays? Flaunt it! Make them blush at your well-roundedness. Give them so many real world examples of your scholastic prowess that they simply can't look away.

Don't, however, make up information. We're talking push-up bra, not silicone injections. Aside from being morally wrong, lying on your application could immediately lead to rescindence of your acceptance, or even invalidation of your collegiate degree if discovered later. Besides, it's much easier to remember what you wrote if it's true.

While your activities list showcases your accomplishments, your application essays should represent your human characteristics. Show them what makes you, well, you, and you'll be well on your way to winning over the admissions counselors' hearts and a hit from their nice green "accepted" rubber stamps.

7. Letters of Recommendation

Letters of recommendation provide admissions counselors the only information about you that isn't written by you, and since letters of recommendation provide unique insight into you as an applicant, it is important to choose your recommenders wisely.

The most vital aspect of taking care of your letters of recommendation is deciding who you want to write them. When deciding which teachers to write your recommendations, it's important to pick the teachers that know your potential. The teachers who push you to succeed will typically make you work harder than most because they recognize talent in you. If you've stepped up to meet their expectations, these teachers can provide great letters of recommendation.

Ask for recommendations early, so your recommenders have plenty of time to write your letter. The more time, the better. Put yourself in their shoes for a minute. You've got hundreds of papers to grade, two accidents to report, and a parent-teacher conference in the evening. Life is trying to crush you, but before you can get out of the class to start working on stuff, some student walks up to you and asks, "Would you be willing to fill out a letter of recommendation for me?" Now, would you, as an ever-swamped teacher, be more likely to write a good recommendation if the student asks you three months before the deadline or one week? Exactly. Teachers are very busy people, so give them plenty of time to complete your recommendation. Not only will your recommendation probably be more comprehensive and organized, but your teacher will probably have an easier time thinking of nice things to say about you.

If you talk to your recommender a few months in advance, you're going to feel the need to ask them about their progress frequently. Don't do it. It's annoying. Yes, it's important that your recommenders complete your recommendations on time, but they don't need a reminder from you every time you see each other. It's probably not their first rodeo, so give them some space. Otherwise, they'll start thinking of you as a modern day tax collector, and dread the arrival of class periods with you. If it starts getting close to the deadline and they haven't said anything about your recommendation, ask them gently if they've gotten to it. If they haven't, don't flip out on them. Just kindly remind them of the due date. As long as you don't treat your recommender like a disobedient teen who keeps forgetting to take out the trash, you'll more than likely end up with a strong recommendation that is completed on time.

A great way to keep your recommenders happy and well-informed is to give them a packet of information when you ask them to write your letter of recommendation. In the information packet, you can include submission deadlines, stamped and addressed envelopes, and instructions for submitting their recommendation. The more streamlined you can make their recommending process the better because the less time they have to spend fiddling with submitting your recommendation, the happier they will be. Make sure you let them know they can ask you any questions about submitting your recommendation and that you are more than happy to help them submit it if they have trouble. The more helpful you are throughout the process, the more charitable your recommenders will feel.

8. Following Up

All right! You've painstakingly developed your activities list, you've written all of the necessary essays or short responses, you've accrued your stellar recommendations, and, after a few breathless moments, you clicked the submit button on your application. You're done! It's time to shoot off the fireworks, do some backflips, pop open the champagne, or drink the milk like they do after that one Indy car race, right? Wrong. Your super close, but don't celebrate before you've crossed the finish line. There's a few more things you can do to give your application the extra boost it might need.

Some colleges use demonstrated interest as a factor in determining admission, and an excellent way to demonstrate interest is to email your admissions counselors with noteworthy activities you've participated in since you submitted your application. Showing the admissions team you've stayed busy even after you sent in your application helps demonstrate your drive.

If you haven't done much since you sent in your app, you can still show interest by emailing your admissions counselors with questions. Ask them about the specific program you're interested in or about internship availability for freshmen. What questions you ask doesn't matter as long as you are keeping your name in front of them. You want to stay on their radar.

Emailing all of your schools' admissions counselors can be a time consuming process particularly if you're applying to a bunch of schools, but demonstrating interest in the school can be what puts your application in the accepted pile if the admissions counselors are waffling. Don't be on the wrong end of the waffle. Follow up with emails after you've submitted your applications.

9. Secondary Applications

If you're gunning for the top scholarship at many colleges, there will be some form of secondary application you must complete to be eligible. Some schools invite all applicants to fill out the secondary application while others only allow a select group to apply. The remainder pulls their scholarship winners out of the regular applicant pool, so no additional application is required. Unfortunately, those schools are the minority, so, if you're trying to get big scholarships, you're probably going to have to do some extra work.

Many secondary applications require students to meet minimum ACT/SAT and GPA parameters to apply. A 32 ACT/1400 SAT I and a 3.8 GPA will allow you to apply for the majority of the high dollar scholarships. If you have a 33 ACT/1450 SAT I and a 3.85 GPA, you can apply to practically all major scholarships. If your numbers aren't that high, don't freak out. There are several schools that don't have minimum ACT/SAT and GPA requirements for their major scholarships, so there are still plenty of opportunities for students with lower numbers to put their hat in the ring.

Most secondary applications also require students to write another essay. Before you go stomping around your room and pouting about your problems, remember that other kids are going to see the essay requirement and decide not to fill out the secondary application. The more hoops students have to jump through to apply for the scholarship, the fewer applicants there will be because many high school seniors are lazy. In fact, many schools purposely make it difficult to apply to their top scholarship program because it deters students who aren't really interested or willing to work. Now, you know their game, so when you see tons of additional requirements on a secondary application you're going to do a happy dance, because you know less serious applicants won't take the time to complete the application, and you will have a better chance of winning.

Much like with the essays for your initial application, it is important that the essays on your secondary applications don't repeat material you've already covered. Your secondary application is your last chance to impress the admissions counselors, so spend as much time on your secondary application essays as your primary application essays.

Once you decide which application method to utilize, fill out your activities list, write your application essays, obtain your letters of recommendation, follow up with your admissions counselors, and complete your secondary applications, the labor-intensive work is over. No more essay writing or application building, so take a breath and relax. Take a nap, play some video games, or do something equally unproductive. You've earned it. You should have a brief period of rest before you have to deal with any more college stuff. If you make it to the final selection stage for a school's major scholarship, however, your period of rest will be cut short, and you'll have to prepare for the most competitive part of the selection process—scholarship weekends.

10. Scholarship Weekend/Interview Tips

College scholarship weekends are the scholastic sphere's equivalent of the medieval tournament's melee, where scores of competitors engaged in free-for-all combat, bludgeoning each other until a few victors remained standing. Though, luckily, most scholarship weekends don't include a brawl, there is a distinct element of competition. Only a few individuals invited to the scholarship weekend will be offered the big scholarship, and most of the students invited will actually have a chance at the big scholarship, so you need to be as prepared as possible for the weekend to maximize your chance of getting lots of money.

When preparing for a scholarship weekend, one of the first things you need to do is prepare to be sociable. For some of you, that's no problem. You can have a delightful conversation with anybody. For the others, however, social interaction might not be your best friend. If you put off getting a haircut because thinking about being stuck in a chair with some barber talking to you for thirty minutes makes you hyperventilate, you're in group two. Unfortunately for the less socially proficient, you're going to have to suck it up and talk to people the entire weekend. You can do it. Just seal yourself in a dark room, curl up in the fetal position, and talk to nobody for the week following the weekend to recuperate if that's what it is going to take, because socializing is an important aspect of all scholarship weekends. Not only will introducing yourself a thousand times prepare you for your interviews, but your hosts could be evaluating how well you interact with others throughout the weekend.

The school putting on the scholarship weekend is going to

end up shelling out a ton of money, so they're going to take every opportunity to make sure they give their money to the right people. Since they don't want to give the money to some chump, they are going to evaluate you at every opportunity, possibly including lunch, or free time, so you always need to be aware. Because you should assume you will always be evaluated during scholarship weekends, you should always be a tad more sociable and respectful than usual. You can deal with a few more pleases and thank yous than usual. Especially since it could help you win dozens of dollars.

Though you may be most comfortable in a sweatshirt and jeans, you should deal with being itchy for a couple days and dress up. You want to show the scholarship committee that you're not some slouch and you're honored to be considered for the scholarship, and dressing up will communicate that you care. You may be a total slouch or think the school should be honored by you showing up, but if you dress well, your interviewers will start off thinking you are taking the interview seriously.

At any scholarship weekend, you will probably have to participate in at least one interview. While there are specific tips for different types of interviews, we will first discuss several tips that apply to all types of interviews.

For starters, you should provide full answers that provide insight into you to your interviewer's questions. If your interviewer asks you "What was the most challenging experience in your life last year?" Don't give a one phrase answer like some angsty high school freshman. Elaborate. Tell your interviewer an applicable anecdote. Now, if your interviewer asks, "Where are you from?" there's no reason to answer in three sections with supporting details for each. You're smart. You can determine which questions should have long answers and which shouldn't.

Don't try to judge how well you're doing by your interviewer's facial expressions. Often, interviewers try to remain expressionless to seem impartial. Whether or not it works is a mystery, but the stoic expression does succeed in scaring many of the kids interviewing, so if your interviewer seems disinterested in everything you say, don't flip out. Just stay relaxed and continue answering the questions to the best of your ability. In actuality, it's hard to tell if you're doing well in an interview. Sometimes, if you think you tanked your interview, you will win the scholarship, or if you thought you killed the interview, you won't get a penny. Don't get stressed if things don't seem to be going your way in the interview room.

Each question your interviewer asks is an opportunity to add another dimension to yourself as a candidate, so you should try to keep your answers diverse in order to provide your interviewer the best image of you. Conversely, if you don't answer your interviewer's questions with diversity, your interviewer will see you as one-dimensional and think you have little to offer the school outside of what you've discussed. Diversity in your answers refers to differing methods of corroboration, not necessarily competing ideas. For example, if all of your answers to the interviewer's questions include your involvement in football, your interviewer is going to think football is all you're interested in even if your application shows you have a variety of interests. Your interviewer is going to remember what you talk about more than what you've written, so make sure to talk about everything you want them to remember.

Several interview questions are so common that you should know how to answer them before you ever step into an interview room. You should be able to belt out answers to these questions in your sleep, and, since these questions are so common, you should be able to formulate some top-notch responses to them. Here are a few questions that all interviewees should be prepared to answer:

"Tell us about yourself."

This is usually one of the first questions that you will be asked in an interview, and you should have a killer response ready, because, since it's usually such an early question, it will set the tone for the rest of the interview. You shouldn't take this question as an invitation to rehash your activities list. Instead, answer the question honestly. Tell them interesting information about your family, you, your passions, and your dreams. Focus on what will differentiate you from the other kids they will be interviewing.

"Where do you see yourself in five years?"
This question boils down to, "Do you have a plan?" Don't jokingly respond with some form of "I've got no stinkin' clue!" That is the wrong answer. Even if you have no stinkin' clue, you have to give them more than that. You've probably thought of what you might want to do and how to get there, so tell them a couple of different routes you might take in detail. If you're pretty set on one particular career, tell them in detail what you plan to do to get there. The more details you present, the more prepared you seem to work towards that goal.

"Give us an example of a time you overcame adversity."
Don't be that goofball who talks about something GPA or ACT/SAT related. Everyone has had to work hard to raise a low grade or improve a test score at some point. Try to talk about something more specific like how you were bullied, your parents' divorce, or growing up as a minority in a super white community. Don't just tell them about how you immediately overcame the adversity, though. Give them the juicy stuff. Tell them how overcoming that particular adversity helped shape your life and pushed you to better yourself—give them the long-term impact.

"Why do you deserve this scholarship?"
This question is a pain because you have to answer tactfully. You can't just say, "Because I'm the bomb ,and the other kids here pale

in comparison to my greatness," even if you are. Instead, acknowledge that there are lots of worthy candidates for the scholarship with great qualifications, but reiterate your strengths and emphasize how they mesh well with the school's mission and environment. Try to think of specific offerings of the school and mention how you plan to utilize them, and even build off of those programs to develop something more expansive.

A great way to practice answering these questions is to mock interview. Knowing what you're going to say to a question in your head is great, but it's a little different trying to articulate your thoughts out loud. Mock interviewing gives you the opportunity to get used to answering the questions you'll be asked in the real thing, which is good, because if you're not used to interviews, the first time you try to answer a question you're probably going to sound concussed. Not to worry, that's why you're practicing. If possible, get a teacher whose opinion you respect be your interviewer, so that when you say something dumb, you can work together to figure out how to prepare a better answer. After a few mock interviews, the real deal will be less of a shock to you, and you'll have a better chance of presenting an excellent representation of yourself through your answers.

Essentially tips for doing well in all types of interviews can be condensed to a few key concepts: be prepared, be on your best behavior, and be relaxed. As long as you remember and execute the key concepts, you will be able to handle just about any interview a college could throw at you. Though general interview tips can give you a good foundation for interviewing, various types of interviews can be further dissected to give you a better understanding of what answers your interviewers are looking for, which would give you a better chance of winning the money. You want a better chance of winning money, right? Swell! Then it's time to delve into some specifics.

11. Individual Interviews (One-on-One)

The one-on-one interview is a pretty run-of-the-mill interview, so if you're going to a bunch of scholarship weekends, you're probably going to encounter this type. One-on-one interviews are typically the interview type of choice for colleges that request students to participate in interviews for admission as well, so if you're dealing with one of those schools, this is probably the interview you'll deal with.

Generally, one-on-one interviews are conducted by a faculty member or a member of the alumni who was asked to squeeze your interview into his or her schedule, so the interview is probably going to be more laid back than other types. Because the interview will probably be laid back, if you start talking about your "academic merit" your interviewer is going to tune you out, and you're going to sound like Charlie Brown's mom.

Just have a conversation. Find a shared interest and discuss the Dickens out of it, because the fewer interview questions they have to ask you the better. If the school gives you your interviewer's name beforehand, take some time to look him or her up and find out what projects they have going on. If you're interested in what they're doing, ask them about it in the interview. Not only will it show that you've looked into the school, but you'll get your interviewer talking about what they like to do, and almost everybody likes talking about themselves.

Your interviewer will probably ask you if you have any questions for them at the end of the interview, and, unless you've thought about it, you're going to be caught with no questions and your mouth hanging open. Think of some good questions to ask beforehand. If you can think of one, ask a question specifically about their department. The closer your questions are related to what your interviewer focuses on, the better the answers they give will be and the happier they will be to give them.

Since one-on-one interviews are more laid back, it is a little easier to tell if your interviewer is genuinely interested in something you say. That's fantastic, because if you notice they seem interested in something you've said, talk about it in greater detail. Don't feel like you need to make sure you tell your interviewer about everything you've ever done. Focus on what you both find interesting so you can have an interesting conversation that you both enjoy. You're looking for quality over quantity in this scenario, so if you only discuss one topic the entire interview, don't flip out. You probably did well.

12. Individual Interview (You with many Interviewers)

Unlike one-on-one interviews, individual interviews with a scholarship board or some other group are more formal. Instead of taking the form of a conversation, interviews with a scholarship board tend to be more question and answer based, so your approach to the interview should reflect the differences. For example, while your goal in the one-on-one interview is to have an interesting conversation with your interviewer, you should focus more on answering the questions the scholarship board asks you to the best of your ability when you have multiple interviews.

Try to do some research on the scholarship board or group that will be interviewing you beforehand. If the scholarship foundation has a web page, make sure to visit it and gather as much information as possible. Read the foundation's mission, if it has one, and read about the past winners of the scholarship. Try to pin down some key characteristics that the committee seems to look for and emphasize interests and involvements of yours that highlight those characteristics in your interview. By doing your homework beforehand and learning which of your involvements and activities to focus on in your interview, you're giving yourself the best chance possible to win the scholarship.

For some reason, scholarship boards or other groups love to ask questions that they think allow them to watch you think on your feet. Most of the time that just means they are going to ask you a couple of dumb questions. However, even though the question may be dumb, you can't show the board that you think it is dumb. If they ask you something like, "If you could fold a piece of paper in half one hundred times, how tall would it be?" Don't just stare at them like they're a bunch of goofballs then shoot off something snarky like, "Probably pretty tall." Is the question a stupid one and would a snarky response not only be super funny but totally warranted? Yes, but you should still do your best to answer even the stupid questions well. The purpose of the dumb questions is to show the committee that you can think on your feet, so give them a show. Play their game and verbally walk them through your thought process for answering whatever dumb question they may ask.

13. Group Interviews (Roundtable)

Group interviews can be incredibly stressful situations if you aren't well prepared. Individual interviews are bad enough, but add other people who are also trying to win the scholarship to the same interview, and it gets a lot worse. One major type of the harrowing group interview is the roundtable. Roundtable group interviews typically consist of a small group of students with one interviewer who poses questions to the group.

Typically, the interviewer asks a question, and every student in the group is given the opportunity to answer. Given the number of students in a single interview, time limits are often utilized to keep the interview length reasonable. Students are usually given a minute or two to respond to each question, and if you're not used to answering questions in a short amount of time, you might not get through everything you want to say or you might cram everything you want to say in too quickly and be forced to sit there awkwardly while the remainder of your time ticks away. Both unfavorable scenarios can be avoided by, you guessed it, practicing. Work with whoever you did for mock interviews and have them set a time limit for your responses.

Your goal when you answer one of the questions is to use up all of the time available. You want to fill up all of your time with information that will help your interviewer better understand you as a candidate, and you want to finish your final thought just before your time expires. Keep in mind that you have a very limited amount of time during a roundtable interview, so it is imperative that you use as much of it as possible.

Since the number of questions and amount of time you will be given to answer is severely limited, you need to focus on keeping your answers diverse. If you're able to, try to only talk about a specific activity or involvement of yours in one or two questions then move on to a different interest or involvement of yours. The more multifaceted you can show yourself to be in the roundtable interview, the better.

14. Group Interviews (Article Discussion)

Article discussion based group interviews are an excellent way for interviewers to see how you analyze and interpret data. Unfortunately, that means you have to be able to analyze, interpret, and communicate your thoughts about the data well under pressure. In an article discussion group interview, you and your fellow interviewees will be given an article to read and discuss in the company of a couple of interviewers.

Interpreting information and sounding smart when you talk about the info is key to acing an Article Discussion Group Interview. Sadly, if you don't have a natural aptitude for that sort of stuff, you also can't do much about improving your lack of ability in such a short time. However, there are some strategies you can employ to mask your lack of skills or make the skills you do have look even better.

One important bit to keep in mind throughout an article discussion group interview is to listen actively. Listen at least as much as you talk. It doesn't matter if you're the foremost authority on the subject you're discussing, don't be that guy who never shuts up. Your interviewers are not going to be impressed if you don't ever let any of your peers talk even if everything you say is golden. Besides, the other interviewers probably have some interesting insight, so actively listen to what they have to say— your interviewers will be evaluating your listening skills as well.

Speak sparingly. Not only does shutting your trap for a couple of seconds show you can listen, but it also gives you time to think of a few awesome things to say instead of spewing a bunch of mediocre stuff. Feel free to express as much nonverbal approval or disapproval as you'd like, but reserve speaking for the times when you can truly add something interesting to the conversation.

Avoid talking about your activities and interests altogether during an article discussion group interview. If you have a personal experience that directly relates to the conversation and will bring up an interesting subtopic, go ahead and share it. Don't, however, try to fit one of your experiences into the conversation if it doesn't relate. Seriously. Going off on some tangent about yourself, that adds nothing to the discussion will make everyone in the interview think you're a raging narcissist, and you definitely won't get the money.

15. Group Interviews (Task Based)

Task-based group interviews represent the pinnacle of interviewing pain. This type of interview is less frequently used, so if you have to participate in one of these interviews, you're one of the unlucky few. In task-based group interviews, usually, the participating students are grouped into a few teams and told to work together to build a tower as tall as possible or some other equally ridiculous task. If the students in the "teams" actually worked together, the task wouldn't be too difficult. Unfortunately, the scholarships are awarded to individuals, so all of the students act as individuals instead of team members.

Just to let you know ahead of time, whatever your team builds is probably going to suck. Everyone is going to try to lead the group, and one guy is going to build whatever he wants to despite the entire group telling him not to. Your ideas, no matter how stellar, are probably going to be ignored, and that one guy is going to break whatever you guys had built in the last seconds and time is going to tick away with everyone bickering and whining like guests on The Maury Show.

If that starts happening in your task-based group interview, and it probably will, don't freak out. Your interviewers aren't looking for who can build the tallest tower. In fact, they probably aren't paying much attention to who has the best ideas either. What your interviewers are going to evaluate during task-based group interviews is your ability to work with others. You want to showcase your ability to listen to other people's thoughts, encourage teammates, tactfully handle dissent, and keep calm under pressure. It doesn't matter if your team finished in dead last. If you demonstrate that you can handle yourself well in high-stress group scenarios, the interviewers will be interested in you.

If you end up with a team member who won't shut up about his terrible idea, don't get frustrated. Instead, pull a page from your preschool teacher's playbook, and hit him with a compliment sandwich. When you were caught eating glue at your desk, did your preschool teacher flip out and abruptly say, "Stop eating glue, fool?" Unless your preschool teacher was Mr. T, probably not. Your teacher probably said something like, "Timmy, I absolutely love your creativity, but glue isn't something you can eat. Your teeth sure do look super white, though!" You can use the same tactic with your stubborn teammate. Just say something like, "Look man, I think you're right about the paper being strong, but I don't think chewing on the pieces then smoothing them out helps the structural integrity of the page. I do think you're right about building a strong base, though, so what if we used the paper as our base?" Even if Timmy just stares at you, then defiantly resumes chewing on the paper in response to your thoughts, your interviewers are going to appreciate your tactful attempt to get your team member back on track.

Task-based group interviews are not evaluated on who builds the best whatever. They're judged on how well the candidates handle themselves in the situation and interact with their teammates. You may have the best idea ever, but if your team doesn't want to do it, you'll be better off listening to your teammates instead of going rogue and doing what you think is best anyway.

16. Following Up (Again)

You just finished up your last scholarship weekend activity which is fantastic because, if you had to tell one more person your name, hometown, and expected major, you were going to have an aneurysm. Now, you can get back to doing crazy things like wearing sweatpants or napping, but, before you go too crazy, you need to do a couple things to keep your name on the minds of your interviewers.

Wait a day before getting back with your interviewers, if you absolutely need a break. Don't wait much more than that if you can avoid it. The scholarship committee is probably going to meet shortly after the scholarship weekend to decide who will receive the big bucks, and you want to make sure you follow up before they make their decisions. All you have to do is send a short email to your interviewers thanking them for their time and expressing your appreciation for the opportunity to participate in the scholarship weekend. That's it. Keep it short and simple. You're just trying to get your name back in front of them, so they have a better chance of remembering you when they're asked if anyone stood out in the interviews.

Try looking for a contacts page on the school website, if you have trouble finding the email addresses of your interviewers. Often, school websites provide the email addresses of their professors, so the information is readily available for students if they have questions. If some of your interviewers weren't faculty and you can't find their email address, let your admissions counselor know you're trying to thank them for their time. They might be able to come up with an address for you. Even if your admissions counselor doesn't end up locating the address, they still might be able to communicate your gratitude directly to your interviewer if scholarship decisions take place on campus.

17. Waiting

You've sent in all your applications and attended all of your scholarship weekends. Unfortunately, you've reached the uncomfortable phase between submission of your applications and notification of acceptance or rejection. While you're in this period of limbo, you are undoubtedly going to get a little antsy— nobody likes waiting for news. You might feel a little irritated by their lack of communication, especially if you keep sending them emails about your recent activities, so to keep yourself from slowly building resentment for the colleges you applied to, there are a couple of meaningful ways you can pass the time.

For starters, you can double-check the status of your applications on the different school websites to make sure they've received all of your required application information. Even if you're sure you've submitted all of your information, the forms are sometimes lost in cyberspace, so it's wise to make sure all of your schools have received the necessary material from you. Luckily, most school websites have a checklist for applicants to see whether the school has received all of the needed forms, so you should be able to tell quickly if your materials have all been received. Schools usually send out confirmation emails to let students know they have received all of the necessary material. After you submit all of the necessary information, give the school three weeks to process your documents, and if they haven't sent you a confirmation email, contact your admissions counselor to make sure your application is being processed.

Make sure you thank your admissions officer for putting up with your stream of questions and information. You may not feel like dealing with emails is that impressive, but when you consider how many applicants your admissions counselor probably had to deal with, the number of emails can add up quickly. Besides, even if they didn't deal with a ton of emails, it's still courteous to thank them for helping you through the application process.

Know your notification dates. The schools you applied to will probably have different notification dates, so keep track of which schools will be releasing decisions on which dates. Don't waste your time checking the school websites for admission notification too early. Just learn the notification date and wait.

When you're waiting for notification from highly selective schools or major scholarship programs, do not assume you got the scholarship or were accepted. Keep in mind that thousands of well-qualified applicants are rejected by highly selective colleges and passed over for major scholarships every year, so you shouldn't expect to be accepted or win the scholarship. Expecting to get accepted or to win the scholarship is setting yourself up for disappointment. However, by treating acceptance into your reach schools or winning the huge scholarship like icing on the cake, you won't be shell-shocked if you end up striking out.

18. What To Do When You Get The News

The days of waiting are finally over. Your admissions decision is one click away, so you hold your breath and shakily click the link to your admissions decision and watch the page, which for some reason loads incredibly slowly, appear with one of three decisions.

Rejected

The decision nobody wants. You opened your admissions decision notification, and the first sentence started, "We regret to inform you..." You gave the school your heart, and they crushed it with one little word. Before you sit down with a few tubs of ice cream and cry your eyes out while watching all of the Youtube videos about the school that rejected you, take a moment to think about your situation. Being rejected from your dream school isn't uncommon. In fact, tons of highly successful people were rejected from their dream schools. Steven Spielberg was rejected by dream school USC's school of cinematic arts twice, and he went on to be the most successful filmmaker in history. Warren Buffett was rejected by the Harvard Business School, but he became the most successful investor of the 20th century, so don't flip out about your college rejections because you're in some good company. If you get rejected, you're not going to attend the school, but you can contact your admissions counselor to get some feedback on what led the selection committee to keep you out of the accepted pool. Then, you might be able to address the mistakes you made on your application for other schools if you hear back early enough.

Waitlisted

This decision can be confusing because the college is interested but not super interested. It's kind of the equivalent of asking a girl out and her saying, "Let me see if these ten other guys are unattached, then I'll get back to you." Unless you're positive you want to date that girl, and you're okay with not being her first choice, don't hang around until she's done talking to the other guys. The same goes for college wait lists. Unless you're positive you're going to attend the school if they accept you, don't accept a spot on the wait list because you're just stringing yourself along. If you do decide that you're going to accept the spot on the wait list, don't twiddle your thumbs while you wait to hear back. Keep them updated with new accomplishments and involvements of yours, and write them a well-crafted letter expressing your commitment to the school and giving explicit reasons for why you want to attend. Also, let the school know what you would contribute to their community that sets you apart. Showing the extra effort will help bump you up a few spots on the wait list, and that might be the difference between acceptance or rejection. If the school decides not to accept you in the long run, don't have a mental breakdown. Be prepared to attend one of the other schools you applied to.

Accepted

Success! You just won the college application game, so do some cartwheels or something else celebratory. Your acceptance notifications are probably going to roll in at different dates; your safety schools will probably be the first to let you know, and they might even try to get you to decide quickly by giving you early decision deadlines. Don't let any of your schools strong-arm you into making a decision before you've heard back from all of your options. Colleges are obligated by law to give you the opportunity to consider your offers of admission and financial aid until May 1st, and colleges that request commitments before May 1st must offer students the opportunity to file a written request for an extension. Unfortunately, the law does not extend to scholarships, so schools can revoke your scholarships if you don't accept by an early date, so you'll have to weigh your options if some of your schools are threatening to revoke merit scholarships if you don't decide quickly.

After you give yourself some time to let your acceptance sink in, check out your financial aid package and scholarship awards to see if you can afford to attend. Being realistic when you pick which schools to apply should help you be able to attend most of the schools that accept you. Unfortunately, there are circumstances in which the net price calculator overestimated your aid, or you applied despite what the net price calculator said and you don't get enough money. These circumstances can quickly cut through the excitement of being accepted. However, if you didn't get the money you needed at a school for whatever reason, you still have a chance of eventually getting the amount of money to make attending the school a possibility.

19. Negotiating with Colleges

If the net cost of attending a school for you is just out of reach, you can try to work with them to bridge the financial gap, but negotiating with your financial aid officer is a very nuanced exchange. Remember, the net cost you were initially presented was formulated by the school's financial aid department, so by saying you need more, you're telling your financial aid officer they screwed up. That's not something most people like to be told, and because of that, you need to be conscientious of what you're suggesting when you ask for more.

Negotiating for more financial aid from colleges is a little like getting a free steak at a restaurant and then asking for a free slice of chocolate cake, so if you're going to try to get more aid, you're going to have to word your request quite carefully. First of all, avoid sounding like you feel entitled to more money. Frankly, the college has tons of other qualified applicants that would be thrilled to have your aid package, so if the tone of your financial aid reevaluation request makes you sound like a whiny toddler, the financial aid officers aren't going to take your request seriously.

Even before telling them that you need more money, thank them profusely for the amount they initially gave you and let them know how much that amount is helpful to you. Also, use very non-accusatory diction, and do not say anything about "negotiating" for more. The financial aid department is not working to give you the best deal; they're trying to make attending the school affordable, so financial aid officers will shut down if you treat your situation like a negotiation. Instead, emphasize your interest in the school and give specific reasons for your interest. Then, when you finally get around to popping the question, say stuff like, "In order to make attending financially feasible…", and give them the specific amount of money you need to make attending a possibility.

In your letter, let the college know about other more generous offers you've received from other schools. Don't make it sound like you're trying to start a bidding war. Just mention that you've received better financial packages from schools X, Y, and Z, and that, while you would rather attend their school, you can't justify going into tremendous debt to attend their school instead of taking the healthy aid package at another school and remaining debt free. Mention the financial packages from schools that have a similar or better reputation than the school you're negotiating with, because if you say you have a better aid package at a less respected school, they aren't going to care. Telling a school like Harvard that they'd better up the ante because you have a better aid package at Lakeside Community College isn't going to be very persuasive.

Though you will still be required to do some serious linguistic acrobatics in your financial aid appeal, there are many schools that readily match the financial aid offers of peer colleges without much protest. For example, Cornell will immediately match the financial aid offers of any other Ivy League school. Cornell does this because they found that students who were accepted to Cornell, but decided to go elsewhere went to peer schools, like Dartmouth, MIT, or Yale because they received more aid at the competing institution. More schools are now following Cornell's lead, and now it is highly common for colleges to match financial aid offers from peer school to try to keep the students.

While using peer universities to leverage other schools is fairly effective when considering financial aid, it is not so for merit aid. Sorry, upper middle-class kids; you're screwed again. Most colleges that match financial aid packages from peer colleges do not match the merit aid offered by the peer school. You can still try to use your merit scholarship at one school to leverage another, but you will be significantly less successful than if you were using a financial aid package as leverage.

20. Making the Final Decision

This is it. You've done all of the work, and now it's time to make the decision. While your decision won't be televised to millions of sports fans like Lebron's was, deciding where you will be taking your talents can still be incredibly stressful. You're not wrong to worry. Deciding which college you're going to attend is a major life decision, and you should weigh your options carefully before you decide.

Wait until all of your schools give you their final financial aid offers before you make your decision. Unless you're in some strange situation, you won't have to make a decision until May 1st, so give yourself some time to mull over the pros and cons of your different offers. It's especially important to give yourself time to think immediately after a scholarship weekend, because the college you're interviewing at will probably be throwing lots of convincing reasons for attending your way. You'll probably leave the scholarship weekend pretty hyped about that school. Give yourself a few days to cool off before you make any decisions. You're not in a rush, so don't to lock yourself in earlier than you need to.

Once you've taken the time to consider all of your offers and you've finally settled on which school you will be attending, let whatever college you've selected know. Call your admissions counselor and have a mini-celebration; then, after you've done everything you need to do to secure your spot at your chosen school, notify your other schools that you won't be attending. Once you let your other schools know you will be going elsewhere, you become the Santa Clause of scholarships because the other colleges can give your scholarship money to other applicants who might need the money to make attending a possibility. Consider letting your other schools know you won't be attending by giving a final thank you to your all of your admissions counselors who communicated with you through your application process. Giving them more time to reappropriate scholarship dollars gives them a better chance of landing stronger applicants.

21. Parting Words

Well, that wasn't too bad, was it? This guide wasn't as painful to read as you thought it would be, right? Either way, now it's time for you to ride off into the sunset with a bit more application process savvy than you originally had. Hopefully, the information in this book gives you a better chance of getting into and being able to afford attending wherever you decide to apply, but that's a secondary goal of this book. The main goal is to prevent the trial by fire that is the college application process, and present you with helpful information that can not only help prevent you from not only blowing your first few college selections, applications, or interviews before actually understanding what you need to do, but can also help you navigate the application process more efficiently so your senior year isn't totally consumed by college applications. Good luck with your applications, and I hope you manage to get through them without too much suffering!

**COMPASS
BOOKS**

Compass Books
PRACTICAL BOOKS FOR WRITERS

**Compass books focuses on practical and informative
'how-to' books for writers. Written by experienced
authors who also have extensive experience of tutoring at
the most popular creative writing workshops, the books
offer an insight into the more specialised niches of the
publishing game.
If you have enjoyed this book, why not tell other readers
by posting a review on your preferred book site. Recent
bestsellers from Compass Books are:**

Write a Western in 30 Days
With Plenty of Bullet-Points!
Nik Morton
Breaking down how to write a Western, including research and
target publishers. Shoot that MS off in a month!
Paperback: 978-1-78099-591-5 ebook: 978-1-78099-592-2

How To Write And Sell Great Short Stories
Linda M. James
Revealing how to write stories that linger in reader's hearts and
minds.
Paperback: 978-1-84694-716-2 ebook: 978-1-78099-362-1

Fiction - The Art and the Craft
How Fiction is Written and How to Write it
Colin Bulman
A highly practical exposition of all the major elements of fiction
– such as plot, conflict, suspense, the hook, inference, character
and dialogue.
Paperback: 978-1-78279-435-6 ebook: 978-1-78279-434-9

Astro-characters
A Writer's Guide to Creating Compelling Fictional Characters
With the Signs of Zodiac
Judy Hall
Offering a unique and easy method of creating effective,
intriguing, and authentic multi-layered personalities that leap
off the page.
Paperback: 978-1-78279-243-7 ebook: 978-1-78279-242-0

Compass Points - A Practical Guide to Poetry Forms
How to Find The Perfect Form For Your Poem
Alison Chisholm
This book shows through a simple, practical approach, how to
enrich your poems through fine structuring of form.
Paperback: 978-1-78279-032-7 ebook: 978-1-78279-031-0

How To Write a Romance Novel
A Beginner's Guide to Getting it Written and Getting it
Published
Susan Palmquist
Find out how to create a unique Romance story with
memorable characters.
Paperback: 978-1-78099-467-3